Lewes Castle

THE CASTLES
OF SUSSEX

Mike Salter

FOLLY PUBLICATIONS

ACKNOWLEDGEMENTS

The photographs in this book were taken by the author between 1971 and 1999. He also prepared the map and the plans. The old prints and postcards are reproduced from originals in the author's collection. Most of the plans are on a common scale of 1:800, although a few buildings such as gatehouses are shown at 1:400 and large buildings and earthworks are generally shown at 1:2000.

AUTHOR'S NOTES

This series of books (see full list inside the back cover) are intended as portable field guides giving as much information and illustrative material as possible in volumes of modest size, weight and price. As a whole the series gives a lot of information on lesser known buildings. The aim in the castle books has been to mention, where the information is known to the author, owners or custodians of buildings who erected or altered parts of them, and those who were the first or last of a line to hold an estate, an important office, or a title. Those in occupation at the time of dramatic events such as sieges are also sometimes named. Other owners and occupants whose lives had little effect on the condition of the buildings are generally not mentioned, nor are 19th and 20th century events or ghost stories, myths or legends.

The books are intended to be used in conjunction with the Ordnance Survey 1:50,000 scale maps. Grid references are given in the gazetteers together with a coding system indicating which buildings can be visited or easily seen by the public from adjacent public open spaces which is explained on page 71. Generally speaking, maps will be required to find some of the lesser known earthworks.

In the companion volume The Old Parish Churches of Sussex there are separate gazetteers for East and West Sussex using the modern boundaries but in this book, with far fewer gazetteer entries, this division was not thought to be necessary.

Each level of a building is called a storey in this book, the basement being the first storey with its floor near courtyard level unless specifically mentioned otherwise.

Measurements given in the text and scales on the plans are in metres, the unit used by the author for all measurements taken on site. Although the buildings were designed using feet the metric scales are much easier to use and are now standard amongst academics working on historic buildings and ancient sites. For those who feel a need to make a conversion 3 metres is almost 10 feet. Unless specifically mentioned as otherwise all dimensions are external at or near ground level, but above the plinth if there is one. On the plans the original work is shown black, post-1800 work is stippled and alterations and additions of intermediate periods are hatched.

ABOUT THE AUTHOR

Mike Salter is 46 and has been a professional writer and publisher since he went on the Government Enterprise Allowance Scheme for unemployed people in 1988. He is particularly interested in the planning and layout of medieval buildings and has a huge collection of plans of churches and castles he has measured during tours (mostly by bicycle and motorcycle) throughout all parts of the British Isles since 1968. Wolverhampton born and bred, Mike now lives in an old cottage beside the Malvern Hills. His other interests include walking, maps, railways, board games, morris dancing, playing percussion instruments and calling dances with a folk group.

Copyright 2000 Mike Salter. First published April 2000.
Folly Publications, Folly Cottage, 151 West Malvern Rd, Malvern, Worcs, WR14 4AY
Printed by Aspect Design, 89 Newtown Rd, Malvern, Worcs, WR14 2PD

The keep at Arundel Castle

CONTENTS

Inside the front cover is a map of buildings described in this book.

INTRODUCTION

Sussex contains some of the earliest examples of the type of defensible residences known to the Normans as castles. In the short period between when William, Duke of Normandy landed at Pevensey in September 1066 and his victory in October over the Saxon King Harold, the Duke erected a castle within the old Roman fort at Pevensey and another on a promontory guarding a harbour at Hastings. Both castles were constructed not of mortared stone but of earth and wood, as was to be the norm for the majority of such fortifications in England for the best part of another century. The castle at Hastings is shown in the Bayeux Tapestry commemorating the successful Norman invasion of England. The palisades were erected from timbers ready shaped for the purpose brought over with the invasion fleet from Normandy. Although their 11th century earthworks have been mostly obliterated by later stonework, Pevensey and Hastings illustrate the two main types of wooden castle built by the Normans. Pevensey is assumed to have been a ringwork, or embanked enclosure, measuring about 80m across on top. The Roman fort was able to serve as a bailey or outer enclosure. Hastings was given a motte or man-made mound with a small palisaded court on top forming a citadel high above two baileys defended by ramparts and ditches facing the one weak side of the promontory. The inner bailey would have eventually contained a wooden hall, chambers, workshops and stores. Here, most unusually, there was a stone-built chapel from the start since a collegiate church already existed on the site before the castle was built, its tower being depicted at the foot of the mound in the view shown on the Bayeux Tapestry.

Motte at Pulborough

Walls of Roman fort at Pevensey

Duke William of Normandy was crowned King of England on Christmas Day 1066 although it took several more years of fighting before all Saxon resistance was quashed, especially in the northern parts of England. He granted estates to his Norman followers in return for specified periods of military service. The Norman lords or barons then in turn gave units of land called manors to their knights, again in return for military service, this system being known as feudalism. The thin veneer of land-owning Normans consolidated their fragile hold on the land by constructing castles serving as residences, strongholds, and status symbols. The Romans and Saxons built purely military forts and defences around settlements but the Normans introduced the idea of powerful individuals erecting fortresses to serve as their private residences and as the administrative centres of their manors. Many of the minor earthworks cannot be dated more precisely than to say they are of some time between the 1070s and the 1140s but more information is available for the more important sites. In addition to Pevensey and Hastings there are three major late 11th century castles all set near the mouths of rivers to command likely landing places of invasion forces. These are Arundel, built by the Montgomery family (whose other main estates were on the Welsh Border), Bramber, built by the de Braose family (also later a major power on the Welsh Border), and Lewes, built by the de Warenne family. All three have mottes, although the layouts vary, Arundel having a motte set between two long baileys, Bramber having a motte isolated within a single large bailey, and Lewes having the very unusual feature of two mottes set at either end of a single bailey, although one motte is rather more dominant than the other. Chichester also had an important castle in Norman times but only a damaged motte now remains.

Keep at Pevensey

For the first two generations after the Norman conquest of 1066 masons were in short supply compared with carpenters and labourers, partly because the Saxons and Danes mostly **erected buildings** of wood except for the more important churches. Buildings of stone took several years of comparatively peaceful conditions to construct so timber was seen as a quicker and easier option when defences were required in a hurry. However timber soon rots when in contact with the ground so eventually wooden structures were replaced with more permanent, and usually (but not always) more impressive stone structures. In Sussex this happened earlier than in other parts of England, and in any case at Pevensey and Chichester Roman stone walls provided part of the defensive circuits of the medieval castles. Pevensey has the base of an early 12th century tower keep with unusual apsidal projections, plus a postern gateway and foundations of a chapel of the same period. It is thought that the flint curtain wall and square gatehouse at Bramber were built before 1100 and that they were then considered so strong that the timber keep on the internal motte was immediately regarded as redundant. In the 12th century the gateway was blocked and the tower above it then became a keep, an unusually isolated one, for the other domestic buildings seem to have been some distance away. It perhaps served more as a court-house than as a lordly residence. The curtain wall around the bailey at Lewes is either of the 1080s or the first quarter of the 12th century, which is the likely date of the shell keep on the higher of the two mounds. This shell keep formed a ring wall with a wall-walk on top and had lean-to wooden buildings inside it. The shell keep at Arundel, one of the best preserved of its type, and one of only half a dozen in England where one can still perambulate the original wall-walk, is probably of the 1130s or 40s. The original round-arched doorway is now blocked. The bailey walls of the same period or a generation later have been mostly rebuilt except for a gatehouse. The walls were flanked by square open-backed towers (also now rebuilt) like those at Framlingham in Suffolk. Arundel also has some remains of late 12th century domestic buildings embedded within the 18th and 19th century apartments. At Midhurst there are footings of an 11th century chapel and a mid 12th century curtain wall, plus a range of buildings, whilst excavations at Aldingbourne revealed one corner of a square tower keep probably of c1120-50.

The 13th century parts of castles in Sussex are very diverse in nature. The most impressive remains are at Pevensey, where there is a gatehouse thought to be of the 1220s. It is a twin-U-shaped towered structure similar to, but slighter than, the contemporary gatehouse built by the Earl of Chester at Bolingbroke in Lincolnshire. The massive curtain walls at Pevensey and their three big D-shaped flanking towers were added in the 1250s and together with the gatehouse form one of the strongest enclosures built in England during the Henry III's reign. At Sedgwick there is part of a polygonal curtain wall around a roughly circular court with one polygonal flanking tower of modest size. Even more modest in size is a square tower at Rye with four round corner turrets containing tiny rooms and a staircase. Only one corner remains of a two storey building probably of the early 13th century at Knepp. Although often described as a keep it seems to have been a hall-house or solar block similar in type to several mid to late 13th century examples in Northumberland, and containing a single public or private chamber over a low basement. In the 1290s Arundel was provided with a twin-towered barbican and a new approach to the keep, whilst several of the flanking towers of the bailey walls were rebuilt. Nothing now remains of an early 13th century hall and little remains of the contemporary ramparts and gateways of the town, nor much of the walls built around Lewes slightly earlier.

Arundel Castle

The barbican and keep at Arundel

When tested by warfare during the medieval period the major Norman castles in Sussex proved to be strong. In 1088 and 1102 garrisons at Pevensey and Arundel had to be starved into submission with lengthy blockades by William II and Henry I respectively, whilst King Stephen failed to capture Arundel in 1139. Pevensey again stood firm against Simon de Montfort in 1264 and Richard II in 1399, but the much weaker castle of Chichester is thought to have fallen to the rebel barons in league with Prince Louis of France in 1216, whilst the abandoned defences of Hastings were over-run by a French raiding party in 1339.

The machicolations on the postern gate at Bodiam

In response to French raids the town of Rye was enclosed by walls by Edward III. Little remains of them except for one quite impressive twin-towered gatehouse, and nothing now remains of a defensive wall built on the seaward side of the town of Hastings. Additions of the first half of the 14th century to older castles are the barbican with two round bartizans and machicolations at Lewes and the undercrofts of two chambers backing onto a D-shaped tower at Bramber. Petworth and Cowdray may have once had fortifications of this period but the only early work of note surviving at either place is a much altered mid 13th century chapel hidden within the late 17th century mansion at Petworth. There are only slight remains of a fortified manor house at Glottenham, the moat being the principal relic.

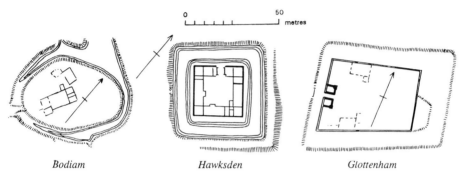

0						50
						metres

Bodiam   *Hawksden*   *Glottenham*

Plans of Moated Houses in Sussex

HERSTMONCEUX CASTLE, SUSSEX

A number of other manor houses in Sussex were provided with moats in the 13th and 14th centuries. Some of them may be a response to periods of unrest during the reigns of Henry III and Edward II, but water filled ditches were not necessarily military in purpose. A moat was a permanent and efficient boundary for keeping vagrants, wild animals and malefactors out of manorial enclosures, and would have been equally useful for controlling the comings and goings of domestic animals, servants and members of the family. At Michelham Priory the provision of a wide wet moat fed by a river seems to have made the usual stone precinct wall unnecessary. At all periods moats have been appreciated as scenic features and they served as a habitat for fish, eels, and water fowl which together formed a substantial part of the diet of the landed classes. A wet moat could also help to drain land otherwise unsuitable for agriculture or inhabitation. Moats were also used to flush away sewage so a house built within one would require a separate source of water for cooking, brewing and washing. Because of the many uses to which they could be put, moats did not require royal consent of the kind required for the erection of embattled walls and towers. However they still had a function as status symbols since only those who held manors or a considerable share of one had the resources to create them.

The words motte and moat clearly have a common origin and although modern historians normally understand them to mean quite different types of earthwork, this was not the case in the medieval period. Although excavations have failed to prove this convincingly, one might expect a gradual development from the conical mounds and ringworks of the 11th and 12th centuries to the low roughly rectangular platforms which are the commonest type of moated site.

Bodiam Castle

Moated site at Pulborough

Sussex contains two of England's finest examples of later medieval castles built on a regular symmetrical plan with wide wet moats. Both are securely dated by the issuing of a royal licence to crenellate. The licence for Bodiam is dated 1385 and specially mentions the fortifications as being necessary against French raiders, whilst the licence for Herstmonceux is dated 1441. Both are almost square in plan with four domestic ranges set around a central court, and each has corner towers, mid-wall towers and a twin-towered gatehouse crowned by machicolations set in the middle of one of the shorter sides. Bodiam has round corner towers and is much the strongest of the two, whilst the corner towers of Herstmonceux are smaller and octagonal. Overall Herstmonceux is larger and more slightly built, the walls there being of brick with stone dressings, and the original hall being in a range thrown across the middle so that its windows looked on either side into courts. In both castles the outer walls have remained almost intact except for crumbling parapets, whilst little has survived of the original inner walls. In 1377 the Bishop of Chichester obtained a licence to crenellate his manor house at Amberley and proceeded to enclose the older house with a curtain wall with a gateway flanked by two round turrets. Rather curiously, the curtain is overlooked by the older church tower.

In the medieval period castle walls of rubble were sometimes limewashed outside, making them look very different from the way they appear today. Dressed stones around windows and doorways would be left uncovered. Domestic rooms would have had whitewashed rooms decorated with murals of biblical, historical or heroic scenes mostly painted in red, yellow and black. Wall hangings decorated with the same themes or heraldry gradually became more common from the 14th century onwards. Although used in churches, glass was expensive and uncommon in secular buildings before the 15th century, so windows were originally closed with wooden shutters. As a result rooms were dark when the weather was too cold or wet for them to be opened for light and ventilation. Large openings in the outer walls sometimes had iron bars or projecting grilles even if high above ground level, as at Bodiam. Living rooms usually had fireplaces although some halls had central hearths with the smoke escaping through louvres in the roof. Latrines are common and indicate which rooms were intended for living or sleeping in rather than storage space.

Furnishings were sparse up until the 15th century although the embrasures of upper storey windows sometimes have built in stone seats, Bodiam having many examples of this. Lords with several castles tended to circulate around them, administering their manorial courts and consuming agricultural produce on the spot. Seats belonging to great lords could be left almost empty when they were not in residence. For much of their lives castles like Bramber gradually crumbled away with only a skeleton staff in residence to administer the estates. Servants travelled with lords and sometimes also portable furnishings such as rugs, wall hangings, cooking vessels and bedding, all kept in wooden chests. The lord and his immediate family plus honoured guests and the senior household officials would enjoy a fair degree of privacy, having their own rooms. Servants and retainers enjoyed less comfort and privacy, sharing of beds and communal sleeping in the main hall and warm places of work like the kitchen and stables being common.

Cowdray House

Camber Castle

The town of Winchelsea has three modest gatehouses probably dating from the early 15th century when Henry V authorised defences for the town. Surviving alterations and additions to older castles in Sussex during the 15th and 16th centuries rare and nothing remains of late 16th century ranges at Petworth. There are a few traces of some late medieval remodelling of the domestic ranges at Sedgwick, but nothing remains from this period at Arundel, whilst Pevensey, Bramber, Hastings and Lewes were gradually used less and less and allowed to fall into ruin. The Ypres Tower at Rye became a prison. There are small solar towers at Rymans in the parish of Apuldram and at Cakeham, by West Wittering, both near Chichester, but neither can claim to be military buildings. As late as 1532 a licence was issued for fortifying the mansion at Cowdray. Although some parts of the house were embattled as allowed by the licence, and it is possible that an older house which once stood on the site was more defensible, the existing house (begun a few years before the licence was granted) has no serious provision for defence. There is one important new military building of this period, however, a blockhouse built to guard the former harbour at Camber. In the 1540s Henry VIII became very nervous of a possible invasion by Catholic forces from France or Spain and had a series of new forts built along the south coast. The blockhouse at Camber was then heightened and given an outer wall with four U-shaped bastions with gunports for large cannon.

Of the sites described in this book only Arundel, Petworth and the towers at Rye, Apuldram and Cakeham have remained continuously habitable. Arundel was much damaged as a result of sieges and slighting during the Civil War of the 1640s and the apartments there are mostly 18th and 19th century work. Petworth was mostly rebuilt at the end of the 17th century, possibly as a result of Civil War damage, although none appears to be recorded. Herstmonceux was dismantled in the 1770s but restored after the First World War. During the Second World War Pevensey saw further occupation by the army, and concrete floors and roofs were inserted into the 13th century towers to allow them to be occupied, whilst the towers of the shell keep at Lewes were remodelled for summer house use in the 19th century. The ruins at Bodiam, Bramber, Lewes and Pevensey, and the still-roofed Ypres Tower at Rye are now regularly open to the public, as is the still privately-owned castle at Arundel.

GAZETTEER OF CASTLES OF SUSSEX

ALDINGBOURNE   SU 923048

Aldingbourne was one of a dozen manor houses owned by the Bishop of Chichester for which Henry VI granted a licence to crenellate in 1447. It is not known whether anything was built as a result of this or the £10 left by Bishop Sherburne for building a new tower. An order for demolishing the castle in 1606 was ignored but it was destroyed by Parliamentary troops under Waller in 1643 and the site sold in 1648. There is little to see at this site now but excavations in 1969 revealed the lower parts of the 3m thick south and west walls of a 12th century tower keep about 12m square. There were slim pilaster buttresses at the corners and in the middle of the side walls. A projection at the west end of the south wall was interpreted as a forebuilding. It appears this keep was slighted either in the 1150s or 70s) and covered with a mound of earth taken from a surrounding ditch and this was then partly surrounded by a buttressed stone wall, a development similar to that of the keep of the Bishop of Winchester's castle at Farnham.

The interior of Amberley Castle

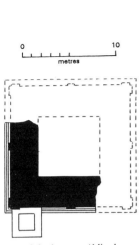

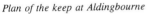

Plan of the keep at Aldingbourne

The gateway of Amberley Castle

AMBERLEY   TQ 027132   V

The castle lies on a low ridge extending west towards what was the navigable upper limit of the Arun. It looks impressive from the south, where there is a curtain wall about 6m high and 87m long rising from a dry ditch and having a gateway flanked by round turrets 5m in diameter. The gateway has a portcullis groove but it does not appear there was ever a drawbridge. The north side is still more impressive, being slightly longer and with the wall rising from a series of low crags. The wall here has loops which lighted a series of lodgings which extended not only along this side but along the 35m long west end and along the south side as far as the gatehouse. On the north is a projection containing twin latrines for these lodgings and there is a wider projection at a slight angle of the curtain. Originally projecting beyond this point was a kitchen block 12m square, but of it only the well recess and service doorway survive. The NE corner is raised slightly for an internal tower containing two storeys equivalent in height to the main wall, plus a lower basement and a fourth storey on top. There was a similar arrangement at the NW corner, but the internal walls there are now missing. Only fragments remain of a central block dividing the castle into a large outer western court and a private eastern court. This block contained a great hall 18m long by 12m wide, of which three service doorways remain at the north end whilst the southern bay and the adjacent undercroft of the former solar are incorporated into a later block. The 52m long east curtain is overlooked by the late 13th century church tower just 7m away from it. This would have jeopardised the military strength of the castle although the church tower may not have then had an open parapet as it has now, and the only opening high up looking out towards the castle is not ideal for archery, whilst the great hall roof would have shielded the main court from any missiles fired from this opening.

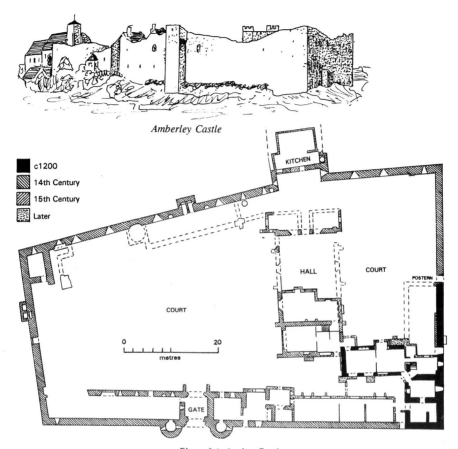

Amberley Castle

Legend:
- ■ c1200
- ▨ 14th Century
- ▧ 15th Century
- ▩ Later

KITCHEN

HALL

COURT

POSTERN

COURT

0 ────────── 20
metres

GATE

Plan of Amberley Castle

The southern half of the east wall is actually the outer wall of a much altered apartment block of c1200 built by Seffrid II, Bishop of Chichester. The original hall block connecting this part with what remains of the late 14th century hall block contains part of a fine Norman doorway of the 1150s, the period of much of the adjacent church. The site was not fortified until Bishop Rede built the curtain wall and gatehouse after obtaining a licence to crenellate from Richard II in 1377. No medieval crenellations survive now, the gatehouse battlements dating only from a restoration of 1908-13, when much of the south side was refaced. Although it has long been assumed the defences were a response to French raids, it has been suggested that the bishop had more to fear from his peasants. The hall and lodgings were built at the same time, and the original hall then converted into a chapel, a piscina of this period still surviving. Alterations were made to the apartments by Robert Sherburne, bishop 1508-36. By the Civil War period the castle had passed to the Lewknor family. It was held by John Goring for the King until captured by Parliamentary forces in January 1644. The great hall was unroofed and furnishings worth £3,000 were sold to James Butler. The castle was later held in turn by the Peachey, Harcourt, and Zouche families until in 1893 it was purchased and restored by the 15th Duke of Norfolk.

Amberley Castle

APULDRAM   SU 844034

In the early 15th century William Ryman built the house known as Rymans south of the church. A three storey solar tower, impressive but of little military value, and now covered with a 17th century pyramidal roof, forms the corner of an L-plan, with a two storey wing on one side and a 17th century wing on the site of the original hall block. The tower and one wing have 15th century windows and the upper storey of the wing has an original fireplace and latrine. The solar in the tower was reached direct from the hall, and a spiral stair at the SW corner then led to a bedroom avove.

Arundel Castle

The shell keep at Arundel

ARUNDEL   TQ 018074   O

Arundel was given by William I to Roger de Montgomery, later Earl of Shrewsbury, and his castle at Arundel is mentioned in 1071 and 1088. It consisted of a mound about 16m high on a shelf above the Arun with one bailey 60m wide extending 80m to the north and a slightly larger second bailey extending southwards towards the river. Roger was succeeded firstly by his younger son Hugh, who was killed fighting the Norsemen on Anglesey in 1098, and then by his elder son Robert de Bellesme, who had inherited the family's Norman estates. In 1102 Robert rebelled against Henry I in support of the king's elder brother Robert Curthose. His castle at Arundel was so strong it could not be taken by force of arms and the garrison only surrendered after being blockaded for three months, the earthworks at Lyminster and Rackham being generally considered to be siege camps erected during this conflict.

The apartments at Arundel

The shell keep at Arundel from the south

When Henry I died in 1135 his widow Adeliza of Louvain came to live at Arundel, which had been granted to her by the king. In 1138 she married William de Albini who was subsequently created Earl of Arundel. In 1139 Adeliza entertained at Arundel her step-daughter the Empress Matilda, who claimed the English throne as the only surviving legitimate child of Henry I. King Stephen blockaded the castle but either through misplaced chivalry or a respect for its military strength he failed to press his attack to a successful conclusion. The shell keep and the curtain walls of both baileys were built during this period. De Albini, who lived until 1176 and also had large estates in Norfolk, is the most likely builder, although Henry I's Pipe Rolls of 1129-30 include expenditure on the castle, possibly the erection of the keep. Expenditure on the castle by Henry II in the period 1176-88 suggests it was kept in royal hands at that time and only reverted to the second William de Albini in Richard I's reign. A new hall was erected in the lower bailey by the 4th Earl, another William, who died in 1224. After his brother Hugh died in 1243, Arundel passed to their sister Isabel's son John Fitzalan, although Hugh's widow probably remained in possession of the castle. When Richard Fitzalan came of age in 1289 shortly after her death he was at last recognised as Earl of Arundel by Edward I. He built the barbican and probably several of the towers. Richard's son Edmund was executed by Queen Isabella and Roger Mortimer after they seized power and deposed her husband Edward II in 1326. They granted Arundel to Edmund, Earl of Kent, but he in turn was executed in 1330 when the teenage Edward III began to rule in his own right, and the castle was eventually restored to Richard, 3rd Earl of Arundel.

Richard, 4th Earl of Arundel, victor of a celebrated naval battle off Margate in 1387, was executed by Richard II in 1397. The castle was given to John Holland, Duke of Exeter, but he in turn was executed by Henry IV in 1400 and the castle was returned to the 5th Earl. The castle saw some use as a prison in this period. It had often been used as such in the 13th century but in the 14th century most prisoners were taken to a new prison built at Chichester. After Henry, 12th Earl, died in 1580 the estates passed to Philip Howard, son of Henry's daughter Mary, who died after Philip's birth. Philip rebuilt the very decayed apartments and in 1584 he entertained Queen Elizabeth I at Arundel. He later incurred her wrath for his Catholicism, being heavily fined and imprisoned in the Tower of London for a decade until his death in 1595. The 14th Earl, Thomas, lost most of his estates under Queen Elizabeth but had them and his titles restored by James I in 1604. In 1642 he accompanied Charles I's daughter Mary to her husband the Prince of Orange and died in Padua in 1646. The castle was occupied by Parliamentary troops but in December 1643 they surrendered to a Royalist force under Lord Hopton. The Royalists in turn were then besieged by Sir William Waller. They can hardly have had time to provision the castle and after a fortnight's bombardment over the new year period which caused much damage they surrendered in January. The castle was then occupied by Parliamentary troops until 1648, when it was abandoned and slighted. In 1660 Charles II restored Thomas, 16th Earl of Arundel, to the Dukedom of Norfolk. The castle was little used during the late 17th century but the 8th Duke repaired some of the apartments. He and his brother, the 9th Duke (1732-77), were imprisoned for involvement in Jacobite plots, the family still being staunch Catholics.

The upper ward at Arundel   *Bevis Tower at Arundel*

Close up of apartments showing Norman windows

In the 1790s Charles, 11th Duke of Norfolk remodelled the apartments in the lower bailey. The library, a late gothic styled room 35m long by 10m wide in the east range, is the principal relic of this campaign. After he died in 1815 the dukedom passed to a distant kinsman, Bernard Howard. A new chapel was built in the 1850s by Henry, 14th Duke, but the existing apartments, including a grand hall in the west range were the work of Henry, 15th Duke, between 1890 and 1903.

As a consequence of all the rebuilding the domestic apartments contain little medieval or Tudor work. Towards the east end of the south front there survives one late 12th century window of two lights with coupled columns and a second blocked Norman window can be traced further west. These may be relics of the chapel mentioned in 1183 and probably recently built by Henry II. Below the hall in the west range is a large Norman tunnel-vaulted undercroft (not seen by visitors) with two north windows now opening into a corridor. In front of or above this undercroft stood an early 13th century hall known to have had a projecting porch with an upper room. Nothing now remains of the late 16th century east range.

Although it is very much rebuilt, the 1.3m thick curtain wall of the upper ward is of 12th century origin, and has various rectangular towers originally open towards the court like those at Framlingham. There is a postern beside the tower at the north corner. The square Bevis Tower with diagonal corner buttresses and shouldered-lintelled windows lying at the SW corner of the upper ward is of the 1290s but with later alterations. There is no evidence that the two wards were divided by a wall. The southern or lower ward has always contained the apartments and the original entrance of the keep faces SE towards it, thus being sheltered from the high ground to the NW. The square gatehouse at the NW corner of the lower ward is often claimed to be late 11th century but the presence of a portcullis groove, a feature not known in Britain so early, makes a mid 12th century date more likely. The second storey has a Norman two light window facing the court but the level above is of the 1290s when a buttress turret was added to the NW corner and a barbican extended in front with a pair of square towers flanking the outer entrance.

The interior of the shell keep at Arundel

The interior of the shell keep at Arundel

Gateway at Arundel

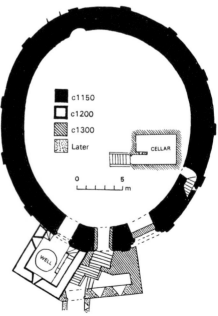

Plan of keep at Arundel

From the gatehouse the curtain wall-walk with a parapet on each side leads up the motte to the shell keep. This has an ashlar-faced wall 2.4m thick with pilaster buttresses rising to the level of a wall-walk 7m above a court 18m by 21m. Within the court steps lead down to a vaulted cellar of the 1290s. Only a few corbels on the shell wall, an upper fireplace of the later medieval period, and part of an oven remain of lean-to wooden buildings two storeys high. The crenels of the mostly rebuilt parapet are tall and narrow and fitted with shutters. The wall-walk is reached by a stair on the east and has a latrine facing north. Facing east is the blocked original doorway with a roll-moulding, chevron ornamentation, and a drawbar slot. The 6m wide well tower on the SW is a later addition although the doorway leading to it may be an original feature once serving as a postern. In the 1290s this tower was given new upper windows, and a projection containing a new entrance with a portcullis groove was added between it and the original entrance. The terrace with two arrow-loops facing south in front of this entrance is renewed work of the 1290s.

The Little Park NW of the castle marks the site of the Saxon burh or fortified town. The east side has a steep natural slope and the other sides were protected by a rampart. On the north are slight traces of a 12th century gatehouse called the Red Gate, part of which stood until 1851. The town seems to have migrated further south by 1295, when Richard obtained A grant of murage from Edward I to pay for the construction of a new rampart which incorporated as its northern boundary the south rampart of the Saxon burh, then provided with a new ditch on the north side. The London road was closed by a new gateway called the Mary Gate after a chapel of St Mary above it. Only one jamb of an arch still remains. The rampart then ran down Mount Pleasant, Parl Place and School Lane towards a another gateway crossing Maltravers Street and called the Marshgate or Watergate, demolished by 1785. The river provided enough defence on the south and the SE section from the bridge to the castle was never closed off.

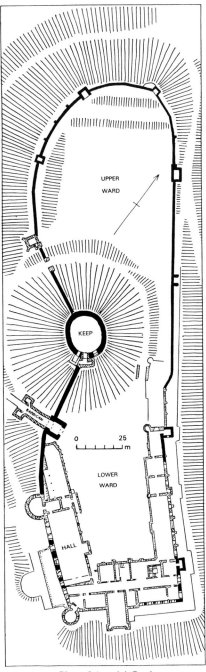

Plan of Arundel Castle

Portcullis at Bodiam

BODIAM   TQ 785256   O

A U-shaped moated site NE of the parish church is assumed to be the site of the original manor house of the de Bodehams and then the Wardeux family. In the 1370s the heiress Elizabeth Wardeux married Sir Edward Dalyngrigge. Sir Edward was licensed by Richard II in 1385 to "strengthen and crenellate his manor house of Bodyham near the sea in the County of Sussex with a wall of stone and lime, and construct and make a castle thereof in defence of the adjacent countryside and for resistance against our enemies". Bodiam lies at the highest navigable point of the River Rother and is assumed to have been built to protect this part of Sussex against French raids. The cost of building it was borne by the riches Sir Edward had amassed whilst fighting in France. The castle later passed to the Lewknor family and in 1483, after Sir Thomas Lewknor had been attainted by Richard III, the Earl of Surrey was ordered to besiege the castle. What happened is not known but the garrison probably surrendered with little or no resistance. The same probably happened during the Civil War, since although no siege is recorded there are traces of a gun platform typical of that period about 250m north of the moat. Bodiam later passed through various families: the Tuftons, Powells, Websters, Fullers and Cubritts, before being sold to Lord Curzon in 1917. The ruins passed to the National Trust on his death in 1926.

The machicolations on the postern gate at Bodiam

The castle lies within a wide wet moat held in by a bank on the south and east sides. Some years ago the National Trust breached this bank in order to drain and clean out the moat and carry out repairs. It has been argued that the castle was little more than a sham folly of little defensive value since if a small modern labour force could breach the bank and drain the moat overnight without the aid of a mechanical shovel then attackers could have done the same. However, they would still then be faced with crossing a wide stretch of mud to get to the walls, no easy feat when under fire. Although the castle's ability to withstand a prolonged attack may be doubted the walls are strong enough and sufficiently well flanked to allow a spirited resistance to have been made against a French naval raid or a local peasant revolt. The moat is now crossed by a wooden bridge from the north to an octagonal platform, from which a drawbridge led into a barbican and then there was another drawbridge in front of the main gateway. Originally the octagonal platform was reached from the west, involving a right angled turn to approach the main gate.

Bodiam Castle

Interior of Bodiam Castle

The castle consisted of four ranges of apartments around an almost square court. Except for around the SW corner the inner walls facing the court are mostly reduced to their foundations, probably the result of dismantling at some time. The outer walls, which are 1.9m thick and rise 12m above the moat, survive complete on all sides, although not much remains of the parapets. In places these walls are pierced by large windows lighting the apartments, and in particular there is a very vulnerable triple lancet in the east wall of the chapel which breaks the symmetry of the layout by projecting on the east side. These windows were all originally fitted externally with iron grilles. At each corner are boldly projecting round towers 8m in diameter and 17m high, only that at the NW corner now being roofed. The towers contain four storeys, the SW tower having a cistern or well at the base and a dove-cot at the top. The SE tower basement was once rib-vaulted and was a treasury or muniment room, Sir Edward Dalyngrigge's bedroom being one of the chambers above it.

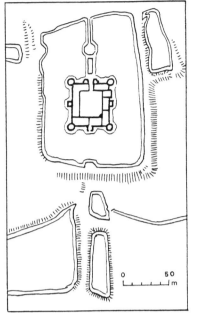

Bodiam: site plan

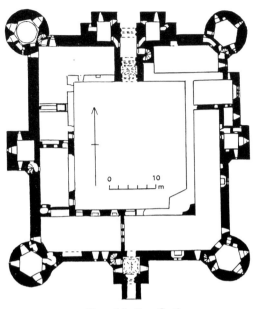

Plan of Bodiam Castle

Towers about 8m wide project 5m from the middle of each of the east and west walls. A similar tower in the middle of the south side contained a postern closed by a portcullis with a short barbican in front of it. This tower has a machicolated parapet with the angles chamfered off, as does the main gatehouse on the north side. The main gate has a central passage flanked by towers of an unusual stepped rectangular form with gunloops of the type with a slighting slot above an oillet. Above the outer entrance are three shields carved with arms. Here an original portcullis, now rather decayed, remains in place. The passage has a rib-vault with murder holes or internal machicolations piercing the bosses. East of the inner part of the passage is a spiral stair still providing access to the gatehouse upper rooms.

Despite the loss of many of the internal walls the disposition of the main rooms is clear. The south range contained the main hall to the east with three doorways in a crosswall to the pantry and buttery and kitchen to the west. Over the low pantry and buttery was an apartment for an important household official. The lofty kitchen still retains its windows towards the court and has large fireplaces in each of the south and north walls. The family apartments lay in the east range, and were of two storeys over a low basement. There was direct access into the chapel, which took the full height of the range. In the NE corner, beyond the chapel, were rooms for guests. A large number of private rooms, each with a fireplace, one or two windows with seats and a latrine, were available in the upper storeys of the towers. The servants had a hall in the west range, partly heated from a fireplace backing onto it in a kitchen beyond. The western part of the north range is thought to have provided stables with a servants' dormitory above.

BRAMBER TQ 185107 F

The wedge-shaped plateau measuring 160m long by 90m wide perched above the River Arun where it breaches the South Downs is a natural site for a fortress. It only required a deep ditch on the west and north sides to make it into a position of great strength. There is no evidence of occupation of the site prior to the de Braose family becoming lords of Bramber soon after the Norman conquest. A castle here is mentioned in 1073 and again in 1086 when de Braose had just dug a ditch to bring water from the river up to the foot of the castle hill. The site was divided into a triangular inner bailey at the north end and a rectangular outer bailey to the south by erecting a motte in the middle of the site. This mound has a summit 24m by 18m and originally had a surrounding ditch. The motte may have been abandoned and its ditch filled in before the end of the 11th century. During that period the whole plateau was walled in with a flint curtain wall 2.4m thick with a wall-walk rising about 2m above the interior but considerably more above the steep slope outside. The curtain wall proved very unstable and required continual rebuilding. A long portion remains on the NW west, with a shorter section further west and another lower part around the SW corner. At the south end was a gatehouse 11.6m wide containing a passage 12.6m long divided into two bays and flanked by walls 2.9m thick. In the 12th century the gate passage was blocked at both ends and the building heightened to 20m to create a four storey tower keep, a new entrance being created through the extra thick curtain wall immediately to the west. Of this keep the west wall containing a passage at second storey level and a window at the third level stands almost complete, and there are stumps of the north and east walls.

East tower of Bramber Castle

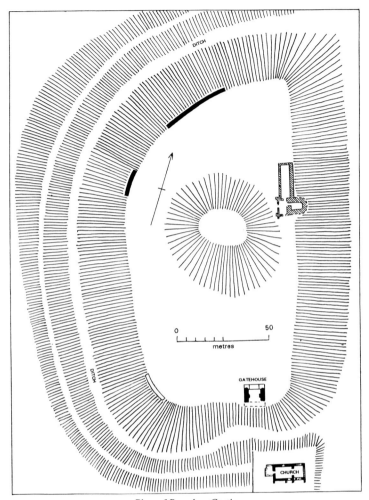

Plan of Bramber Castle

By 1206, when he fell out with King John, William de Braose was one of the leading lords of the kingdom, with possession of 16 castles, most of them in the Welsh Marches. The jealous king starved William's captive wife and son to death, and the family only regained their honours after Henry III succeeded to his father's throne in 1216. In 1326 Bramber passed to the Bohuns and then in the 1330s to the de Mowbrays. On the east side of the plateau are the lower parts of two undercrofts of apartments and a U-shaped tower, all probably of about this period. The de Mowbrays were initially absentees but as a result of a recent French raid Edward III in 1338 ordered John de Mowbray to live at Bramber and make the castle secure. Despite this two French pirates captured at Shoreham in 1355 managed to escape from imprisonment in the castle. Fear of French raids instigated the locals to petition Richard II to order the fortress to be garrisoned and kept in repair in the 1380s. The last recorded constable seems to have been Robert Langton, appointed in 1447.

Curtain wall at Bramber Castle

Apartments at Bramber Castle

The Mowbrays successors the Howards held Bramber until it was sold in 1925 but they lost possession for a short while when out of favour in the 1550s. A reference to the "late castell" then when Edward VI sold Bramber to Edward Leukenor suggests that the building was then ruinous. It is quite likely that by then the south wall of the keep had collapsed through instability of the steep slope in front of it, making the castle untenable. There is no certain evidence that the site was used or harmed during the Civil War although a skirmish took place by the bridge below it, a Parliamentary force having created a strongpoint there. A drawing by Hollar made in the 1650s or 60s shows the keep complete except for the collapsed south wall and this has given rise to a suggestion of slighting, for which there is no evidence. The National Trust purchased the site in 1946 and it was excavated in the 1970s.

BRIGHTON

An Elizabethan artillery blockhouse by the shore was destroyed by the sea in 1761.

CAKEHAM   SZ 784976

This manor house of the Bishops of Chichester was described as ruined in 1363. Bishop Adam Moleyns was granted a licence for crenellation by Henry VI in 1447 but the three storey tower of little military value was built by Bishop Robert Sherburne between 1508 and 1536. The upper storeys are reached by a stair in a turret. Adjoining is part of the vaulted undercroft of a 13th century hall 14.5m long by 6.5m wide, with just a fragment of the hall itself now remaining.

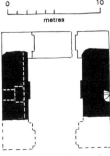

Bramber: gatehouse plan

The gatehouse, Bramber Castle

The central tower of Camber Castle

CAMBER   TQ 922185   V

In 1486 Sir Richard Guldeford was granted the lordship of Higham on condition of building a tower to defend the mouth of the river Rother, then a useful port. It seems that nothing was actually built until 1512-14, when a round blockhouse 20m across over ashlar-faced walls 3.3m thick pierced with gunports was erected by Sir Edward Guldeford, much of the cost of £1,300 being borne by the Treasury. Between 1539 and 1543 Henry VIII spent another £15,750 on greatly strengthening the site, 1,272 men being busy there in 1539 under the command of a mason called John Molton, although the surveyor Steffan von Haschenperg designed the works. The blockhouse was heightened to the height now marked by the original stringcouse of 1514 then reset. It became a keep surrounded by an octagonal court 45m across entered through a rectangular gatehouse on the NW side. The court was enclosed by double walls within which were vaulted chambers with loopholes towards the court, whilst the outside seems to have been covered by a glacis of earth and shingle. A narrow vaulted passage was build around the keep, and from it passages led to out to three storey towers which were square towards the field and round towards the keep. In front of these towers lay earth bastions containing long rectangular vaulted chambers. The building thus completed in 1540 was drastically modified in 1542-3. The keep was given another storey, a D-shaped outer part was added to the gatehouse, the glacis was removed and the outer wall thickened externally and heightened, whilst the bastions were rebuilt as massive D-shaped structures 18m across built entirely of stone and containing gunports. The shingle site required massive foundations for these works and prevented the digging of a moat.

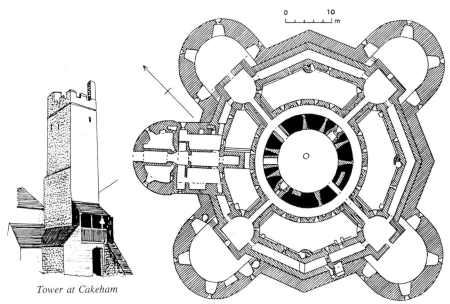

Tower at Cakeham

Plan of Camber Castle

In July 1544 a garrison of 8 soldiers and 6 gunners was installed under Philip Chowte, the number of gunners having risen to 17 by 1550. Elizabeth I spent £170 on repairs in 1584, but by the 1620s the river had moved out of range of the castle guns, and in 1642 the guns were removed to Rye and the castle was dismantled. Although the internal details are rather ruined the outer curtain and bastions all remain standing to their full height external height of 8m to the wall-walk. The much-altered keep also remains mostly intact and rises 14m above the ground outside.

Camber Castle

Roman city wall at Chichester

CHICHESTER   SU 863052   F

In the late 2nd century AD the Roman town of Chichester was provided with a rampart with a stone outer face about 3m high and a ditch enclosing an irregularly shaped polygonal area. Much of these defences remain intact, especially on the east, and on the west and north where there are boldly projecting U-shaped solid bastions about 4.5m wide added a century later. The four gateways facing the cardinal points were rebuilt in medieval times but removed later to ease traffic flows.

In Priory Park, within the NE corner of the city walls, is a modest oval motte, probably somewhat reduced from its original form. It rises 4m above the surrounding playing fields to a summit 12m by 30m. There was probably a bailey extending from it to the city rampart. A chapel in the castle here is mentioned in 1142. The castle was garrisoned in 1193-4 and a prison built in 1198-9. The castle is assumed to have been captured in 1216 by Prince Louis of France, but in 1217 it was recaptured by a royalist force under William Marshal and then destroyed. In 1222 there is mention of the vacant site being illegally used by the Dean and Chapter of the cathedral.

After a fire in 1187 Bishop Seffrid II provided his palace with a new hall and chapel, later altered and then encased in brick in 1725-7. Other ranges are 15th and 16th century and there is a fine medieval kitchen. The palace is approached through a fine early 14th century gatehouse but there is no evidence that it was defensible.

The castle mound at Chichester

Cowdray House

COWDRAY SU 891217 V

The original seat of the de Bohuns in this district was Midhurst Castle, which was destroyed by the Earl of Arundel during Edward II's reign when John de Bohun was a minor in the earl's custody. It appears that the Bohuns had already established a second house nearby and this must be "la Coudreye", a manor house broken into by malefactors, according to a complaint dated 1320 by Joan, widow of John de Bohun. At some point this house was provided with a moat, either in the 1270s or perhaps in the 1320s in response to the recent raid. After another John Bohun died c1492 Cowdray passed to his daughter Mary, who married Sir David Owen. In the 1520s he is thought to have begun the existing house. It has four ranges around a court 37m by 33m, the hall being in the middle of the east range with the private apartments north of it. The service rooms lie to the south and a polygonal-ended chapel projects to the east, while a porch covers the entrance from the courtyard. A gatehouse with octagonal corner turrets lies in the middle of the west range and the SW corner is built up as a rectangular tower, whilst the north range contains on the upper storey a long gallery with polygonal central bays projecting north and south.

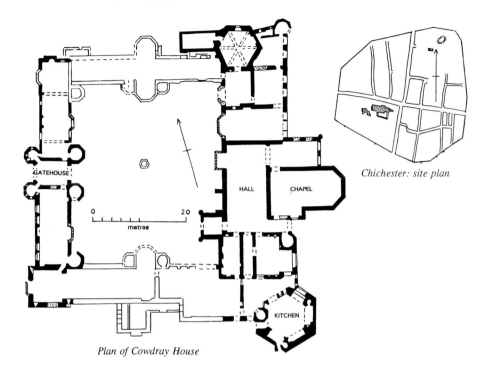

Chichester: site plan

Plan of Cowdray House

The hexagonal towers at the NE and SE corners are probably the work of Sir William Fitz-William, who purchased Cowdray in 1529, although Sir David Owen remained as a tenant until he died in 1535. The NE tower has a vaulted basement, off which leads a later wine cellar. The SE tower is larger and contains a kitchen which recalls the late 15th century hexagonal kitchen at Raglan Castle in Gwent. In 1532 Sir William obtained a licence from Henry VIII to build "walls and towers" at Cowdray, and to "battle and fortify, crenellate or machicolate" the house. By the time of King Henry's visit in 1538 Fitz-William had been created Earl of Southampton, held the offices of Lord Privy Seal and Lord High Admiral and had made Cowdray into a very princely seat. It was probably then still moated, although no trace of this feature survives today. When Sir William died in 1542 Cowdray passed to his half brother Sir Anthony Browne, whose son of the same name was created Viscount Montague by Queen Mary in 1554. The father was more interested in converting Battle Abbey into a mansion but the son lived at Cowdray, and the upper parts of the gatehouse and the windows of the western range are thought to be his. The second Viscount provided the private apartments with bay windows towards the court c1600.

In the 18th century the 6th Viscount inserted a number of new windows. Shortly after the 8th Viscount drowned whilst shooting rapids on the Rhine near Laufenburg in 1793 the house was accidentally destroyed by fire. Elizabeth, the heiress and her husband William Poyntz transferred to the Keeper's Lodge in the park. This family sold Cowdray to Admiral George James, 6th Earl of Egmont. In 1908 the estate was sold to Sir Weetman Dickinson, created Baron Cowdray in 1910 and then made Viscount Cowdray in 1917. He had the ruins of the old mansion consolidated in 1909-14 and in the 1920s it was opened to the public.

Cowdray House

EDBURTON   TQ 238110

High up above the north-facing slope of the South Downs is a worn down motte now hardly rising above the level of a bailey about 50m across in each direction to the north of it. The bailey has a substantial rampart, ditch and counterscarp bank.

GLOTTENHAM   TQ 726221   V

Excavations on the platform of this moated site partly cut in rock have revealed traces of a 0.9m thick curtain wall around a court 60m by 40m, evidence of buildings inside, and footings of a gatehouse with two square towers projecting within the west side of the court. By 1299 the manor had passed from the de Glottenhams and was held by Robert de Etchingham. He built the walls in the 1320s and died in 1327, one year after inheriting his elder brother William's estates. The house thus became a secondary residence of the head of the family and was subsequently little used.

Cowdray House

Hastings Castle

HASTINGS   TQ 647104   F

The Bayeux Tapestry depicts the construction of a motte at Hastings just prior to Duke William of Normandy's victory over King Harold in 1066. The tapestry shows on the mound a citadel built from timbers fashioned in Normandy and brought across with the invasion fleet to help establish a Norman bridgehead on the south coast. The motte lay at the NE corner of a rectangular bailey, on the north side of which was a collegiate church which had been founded by Edward the Confessor in memory of his younger brother Alfred, murdered in 1037. The new castle was given to Humphrey de Tilleul, but he permanently returned to Normandy in 1069 after his wife protested at his prolonged absence. From then until 1088 the castle and lordship were held by Robert, Count of Eu. Archbishop Anselm preached in front of King Stephen in the church in the 1130s and Thomas Becket was dean of the college in the 1160s.

Work on the castle is recorded in Henry II's Pipe Rolls for 1160-1, 1170-4 and 1181-3, but exactly when the bailey was walled in stone remains uncertain. Nor is it known who built the keep which existed by the 1170s but has now vanished. King John ordered the castle demolished but it remained in use as a fortress throughout the 13th century. There were conflicts between the garrison and clergy, the place being abandoned to the latter in the 1331s, only to be refortified by Edward III after a French raid in 1339 when the castle was captured without resistance. The castle was attacked during a local revolt of 1366 and there was another serious French raid in 1377. It was probably during this period that about half of the bailey fell into the sea. The site was later held by the Pelham family but probably only used by the clergy until the college was dissolved in the 1540s and the place abandoned.

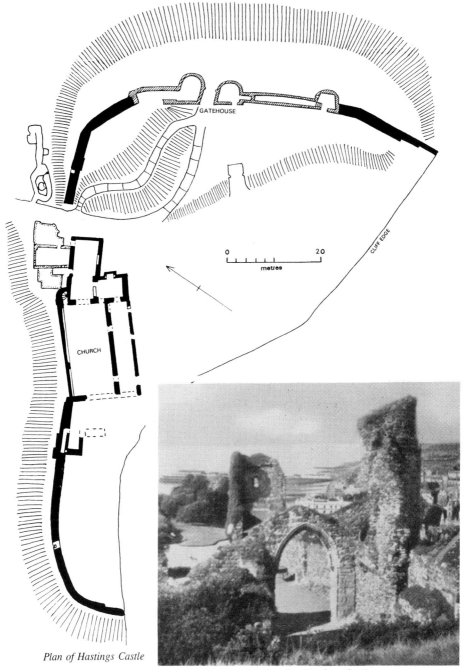

GATEHOUSE

CLIFF EDGE

0   20
metres

CHURCH

Plan of Hastings Castle

The chapel at Hastings Castle

The remains exhibit some curious and puzzling features. The collegiate church has a wide nave with a central tower and chancel very irregularly laid out, these eastern parts bending considerably to the south. There is a south transept with a recess for an altar, whilst on the north side of the tower there is no more than a stair turret. A chapter house projects north from the chancel. On the south side of the nave and communicating with it by two doorways is what is thought to have been a cloister alleyway. West of the nave was a narthex or porch with two towers projecting west. Only the northern tower survives. It has a latrine and, like the thin nave north wall (rebuilt in the 1820s), formed part of enceinte of the bailey defences. From this tower a long section of 1.5m thick walling curves round the NW corner of the site. The rebuilt pointed arch between the central tower and nave can hardly be earlier than the 1190s, and the narthex, NW tower and curtain may also be of that period.

A bank and ditch closed off the eastern side of the bailey from the high ground to the east, where there was an outer bailey known as the "Ladies Parlour" and yet another enclosure beyond. The motte at the NE corner is now no more than a part of this bank. A curtain wall 1.8m thick standing up to 2m high runs across the motte site round to a gateway passage with a portcullis groove flanked by two very thinly walled D-shaped towers about 5.5m in diameter. Another section of curtain, or rather two very thin walls flanking a passage, connects the southern gateway tower to another smaller tower and then runs on to the cliff edge. These weak eastern defences are probably 13th century, but the walls may have been thinned internally sometime in the 18th or 19th century. Immediately north of the motte and opening off the path leading to the destroyed gateway between the motte and the church (i.e. outside the castle walls) are passages connecting three cells carved in the rock. Commonly described as dungeons, their date and real purpose is unknown.

The town lies in a valley between the castle and another headland to the east. Nothing now remains of a sea wall built in the late 14th century to close off the seaward approach and prevent French raiders landing and advancing up the valley.

Remains of the gatehouse at Hastings Castle

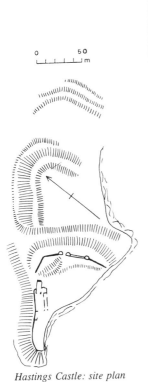

Hastings Castle: site plan

The gatehouse at Herstmonceux Castle

HERSTMONCEUX TQ 647104

In Norman times the manor belonged to the Herst family from Monceux near Bayeux. A Herst heiress married Sir John de Fiennes in 1320. Their great-grandson Sir Roger Fiennes fought at Agincourt, was Treasurer of the Household to Henry VI and became Lord Dacre. In 1441 the king licensed him to crenellate his house at Herstmonceux, and the existing palatial building is the result. One of the Leonard family married an heiress c1600 and took the Dacre name and title. One of their descendants married the illegitimate daughter of Charles II and the Duchess of Cleveland but he got into financial difficulties and had to sell the castle to a Mr Naylor for £38,215. It later passed to Dr Hare, Bishop of Chichester, and a new house, Herstmonceux Place was erected to the NW. In 1777 Dr Hare's second son Robert had the internal walls of the castle dismantled and it remained a ruin with the moat drained until restoration was begun for Colonel Lowther in 1913, and then continued by Sir Paul Latham in the 1930s. In 1948 the Royal Observatory transferred to Herstmonceux from Greenwich and several large telescopes have been built in the grounds.

Air view of Herstmonceux Castle

The castle lies within a broad wet moat, now dry at the north end. It was a stronghouse rather than a fortress, not easy to break into or get out of but not able to withstand a siege. It measures 60m by 57m externally and is of brick with stone dressings. The outer walls are barely a metre thick and although embattled were pierced by two levels of quite large openings, the lowest being 5m above the moat. Boldly projecting from the corners are octagonal towers 5m in diameter. In the middle of the east, west and north sides are half-octagonal towers of similar size, that on the north containing a postern gateway with an incomplete barbican in front, whilst that on the east contains the sanctuary of a chapel. Between these middle towers and those at the corners are smaller and lower half-octagonal towers 4m in diameter. None of these towers have any shooting loops but there are gunloops, cross-loops and machicolations on the impressive twin-towered gatehouse on the south side, reached by a long bridge across the moat. The gatehouse towers are octagonal below but round higher up, and round again but of smaller diameter above the machicolated parapet. The gateway passage has a fine lierne vault and, very unusually, a fireplace.

Prior to 1777 there were not only two storey ranges on each side as now but a range running east-west across the middle containing a great hall backing onto private apartments in the east range, from which the chapel was reached. From the service end of the hall a passage led north to the postern gate, creating two smaller courts beyond the hall range. There is now just one large impressive court with a great hall of 1913 in the middle of the west side. Older rooms survive only on each side of the two gateways, but they and some of the 20th century rooms contain 16th and 17th staircases and other old features brought in from other houses.

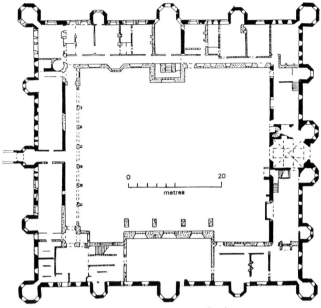

Plan of Herstmonceux Castle

Old picture of Herstmonceux Castle

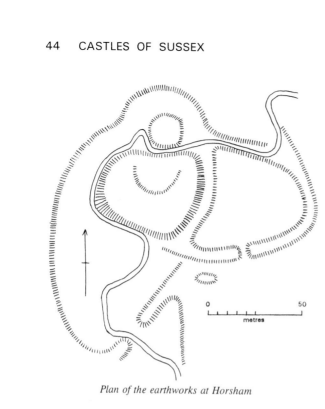

Plan of the earthworks at Horsham

Herstmonceux Castle

Castle earthworks at Horsham

HORSHAM TQ 188333 V

Within one of the many bends of the stream known as the Channelsbrook 2km north of Horsham are earthworks of a castle either built by William de Braose or his son Philip. The remains consists of a much damaged ringwork about 45m by 30m with to the east a slightly larger shovel-shaped bailey defined by a ditch 10m wide. The causeway across the bailey ditch is thought to be later and that the original outer entrance was closer to the ringwork. The ditches were water filled, those protecting the ringwork being 15m wide but extending into a triangular pool held back by a dam south of the ringwork. Either after Philip de Braose was banished in 1110 or perhaps when many adulterine castles were demolished after the accession of Henry II in 1154 the castle seems to have been slighted and abandoned. The dam was breached and part of the north side of the ringwork tumbled into the moat, diverting the stream out beyond it until floodwater later cut a new path through the neck of the blockage.

IDEN TQ 900239 V

The well preserved rectangular wet moat at Moat Farm may date from about the time of a licence to crenellate the manor house issued to Sir Edmund de Passeley by Edward II in 1318. The platform is entered by a causeway towards the north end of the west arm of the moat. After 1420 William Swynburne held two thirds of the manor but the Passeleys recovered it and in 1460 conveyed it to John Scott. It passed in the 1650s to Sir Nathanial Powell and in 1769 went to Catherine Owens.

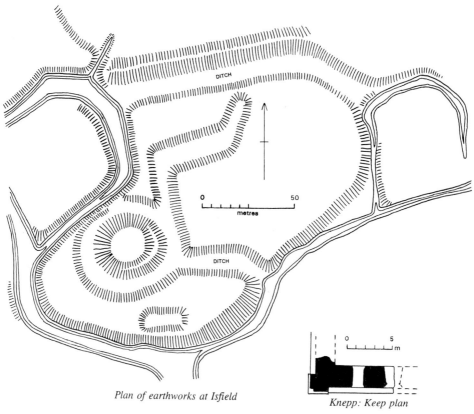

Plan of earthworks at Isfield

Knepp: Keep plan

ISFIELD　TQ 443180　V

West of Isfield church is a low motte 15m across on top with a surrounding ditch, a 90m long outer bailey of 10 acres to the east and a crescent-shaped inner bailey 20m wide and 100m long on the south side. The earthworks, especially the ditches, are now very overgrown and although they seem rather feeble the site is actually quite strong. The rivers Ouse and Uckfield meet on the south side of the site and originally both rivers had loops enclosing the entire site except on the north where there is a ditch 18m wide, presumably once water filled.

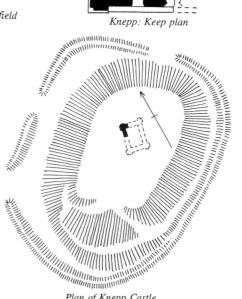

Plan of Knepp Castle

Knepp Castle

Knepp Castle

KNEPP   TQ 163209   V

To the west of the A24 is a low natural platform probably once surrounded by water or marshes. Upon it stands one corner of what seems to have been a two storey hall-house or solar block with walls 2.3m thick above a plinth and pilaster buttresses, the lower part of the remaining ones having been rebuilt. There is a round-headed doorway and a jamb of a large upper window. Several corbels remain from a corbel table which carried a parapet. Knepp belonged to the de Braose family and was used as a hunting lodge by King John in 1206 and 1214. During the crisis of 1216 he ordered Knepp to be destroyed to prevent the rebels using it since the place was not regarded as strong enough to resist them. The wooden outworks were to be taken to Dover. The surviving fragment is likely to have been the work of Walter de Braose, to whom Henry III returned Knepp in 1218. By 1282 the place was held by the Cnap family and it was later held by the Mowbrays and Seymours, but the house (Knepp is never referred to as a castle in the medieval records) probably saw little use after the early 14th century. The Burrells built a house nearby in 1752.

The motte of the first castle at Lewes.

LEWES   TQ 416097 & 414102   O

A terraced mound 8m high and 15m across on top beside a bowling green beyond the station south of the town is the site of the original seat here of William de Warenne, a follower of William I who served as a Chief Justiciar in the 1070s. The site was later given to the Cluniac priory he founded to the west in 1077 and William then transferred to the existing castle site much higher up in the NW part of the town. For his support of William Rufus in 1087 William was created Earl of Surrey but he died after being wounded whilst serving with the royal army in the siege of Pevensey in 1088. The second Earl was a minor when he succeeded his father. He initially opposed Henry I but was soon restored to favour and fought for Henry at Tenchebrai in 1106. He probably built the shell keep some time between then and his death in 1138. The third Earl, another William, fought on each side in turn during the civil wars of the 1140s, only to be killed by the Turks whilst on crusade in 1147.

Old print of Lewes Castle

Isabella, daughter of the 3rd Earl, married firstly King Stephen's younger son William of Blois and then secondly in 1162 Hamelin Plantagenet, an illegitimate half brother of Henry II. Hamelin lived until 1202 and is notable as the builder of the fine castle of Conisborough in Yorkshire but no work at Lewes is assigned to his period. The polygonal towers added to the shell keep were built by John, 7th Earl of Surrey, who succeeded at the age of four in 1240 and lived until 1305. His colourful life including fighting on both sides in the wars of 1263-4, being fined £10,000 marks for an attack upon Alan, Lord Zouch and his son in Westminster Hall c1268, being granted the additional title of Earl of Sussex by Edward I in 1274 and taking a leading part in the English campaigns against Scotland in the 1290s. A third earldom, Strathearne, was granted to John, 8th Earl, for services in support of Edward Balliol during his short-lived rule as King of Scotland. This earl added the barbican in front of the main gatehouse and died in 1347. He was excommunicated for deserting his wife Joan and his only children were those of his mistress Maud de Nerford. His estates passed to Richard Fitzalan, 13th Earl of Arundel, son of Alice, sister of the 8th Earl of Surrey. The Earl of Arundel had several residences scattered across England. When in Sussex he stayed at Arundel so Lewes castle was left empty.

In 1382 several of the townsfolk broke into the castle and destroyed records stored within it. After the 15th Earl of Arundel died in 1415 the barony of Lewes was shared between his sisters, married to the Howard Dukes of Norfolk, the Stanley Earls of Derby and the Neville lords of Abergavenny. Two of these families still have shares, but the Stanley share passed to the Sackvilles and in the 20th century was held by Earl de la Warr. Much of the castle was dismantled in the 1620s. The wool merchant Thomas Friend purchased the barbican in 1733 and the keep in 1750. They later passed to Thomas Read Kemp. The keep became the museum of the Sussex Archaeological Society in 1850 and it and the barbican are now held by the Sussex Archaeological Trust, whose museum now adjoins the barbican.

The shell keep at Lewes

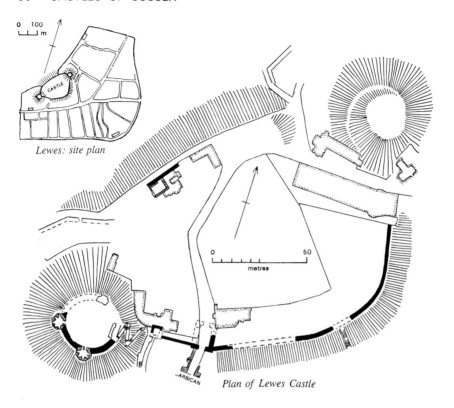

Lewes: site plan

Plan of Lewes Castle

The town of Lewes is roughly a triangle with the SE corner rounded off and the north and west corners cut off. Parts of the town walls built between 1266 and 1275 survive here and there but the gates facing east, north and west have been destroyed. The west gate had a passage flanked by D-shaped towers 7.5m wide containing guard rooms each with three arrow-loops towards the field and a latrine at the side. The castle lies in the middle of the NW side and comprised an oval bailey platform 130m by 110m with the unusual arrangement of a motte at each end. The most likely reason for this is that William de Warenne's wife Gundrada was a lord in her own right, and thus entitled to her own status symbol keep. The mottes are composed of roughly square chalk blocks and could have borne the weight of shell keeps immediately but since no other shell keeps are known to be this early a 12th century date is perhaps more likely. The eastern motte is known as the Brack Mount and has an overgrown summit 17m across rising only slightly above the bailey, which here slopes down to create a depression between the two. Nothing now remains of any stone structures on the summit. Either in the 1080s or c1110-35 the bailey was enclosed by a wall up to 2.5m thick and 5m high on the outside. Fragments of it remain on the east and south sides with traces of herringbone masonry confirming the early date. The only towers are the gatehouse and a now very ruinous tower about 6m square where the wall ran up to the east side of the western motte. The bailey now contains several houses, a bowling green and a former brewery now used as the East Sussex Record Office. Some vaulted cellars under the house called Castle Precincts on the north side of the bailey are the only relics of any domestic buildings.

0   5
m

2nd STOREY

Lewes: barbican plans

The Barbican from the Moat, Lewes Castle

The barbican at Lewes

Only the east and south walls now remain of the gatehouse. It was a substantial structure roughly 12m square, i.e. comparable with the gatehouse-keep at Bramber. Two walls extended in front out to the barbican, although the eastern wall is now missing. The western wall bears a wall-walk from which is reached a stair in a small round turret on the barbican NW corner. The barbican has a rib-vaulted passage with a portcullis groove in the innermost arch. Blocks of masonry about 3m square adjoin both sides and support bartizans 3.7m in diameter containing small rooms opening off the second and storey third main rooms over the gate. At the second storey level there are cross-loops with bottom roundels in both bartizans and in the walling over the outer gateway. The third storey room has an ogival-headed window tucked under the machicolated parapet extending between the bartizans. The eastern bartizan does not survive to this level, and that on the west has been rebuilt without openings.

The shell keep on the western motte took the form of a wall 2m thick above a stepped plinth and rising to a wall-walk 6.6m about the court, which was an oval of 26m by 24m. The southern half survives almost complete with worn battlements remaining at the east end. On the east there seems to have been some sort of rectangular entrance tower and towards the west and south are late 13th century polygonal towers 7.5 wide. To the tops of their parapets these towers rise 11m above the court, whilst towards the field each has a broad splayed plinth descending another 5m. Originally each tower contained a room at court level with an arrow loop in each of the five sides facing the field and an upper storey with the unusual arrangement of an arrow loop piercing each of the four outer corners. The south tower now has an intermediate level, but if such rooms originally existed they were low, without light and perhaps reached only by trapdoors. The entrances to both towers, the windows replacing some of the arrow loops, and the staircase in a round turret behind the south tower date from when the keep became a summer house in the 19th century. Of the internal buildings the only relics now visible are a few corbels and a fireplace in the section of the shell wall between the two towers.

The keep at Lewes

Air view of Mitchelham Priory

The keep at Lewes

Gatehouse at Mitchelham Priory

The gateway at Lewes Castle

LINDFIELD   TQ 356261

A mound west of the River Ouse may be a worn down motte.

LODSWORTH   SU 934210   V

Squeezed between a lane and the east bank of the Rother is a mound rising 6m to a summit 16m by 14m across. Excavations found 13th century pottery shards on the summit plus trenches probably for the cross trees of the base of a later windmill.

MICHELHAM   TQ 559093   O

The site of the Augustinian priory founded in 1229 is a large rectangular platform surrounded by a wide wet moat through which flows the Cuckmere River, an arrangement secure enough for the priory to be classifiable as a stronghouse. The only ancient access is by a 16th century bridge leading to a fine 15th century gatehouse with two storeys of rooms above the passage flanked by lodges. There are two light upper windows facing NW towards the moat but no windows face SE to the court, only a staircase turret. Nothing remains of the priory church but the existing house incorporates the refectory on the south side of the former cloister and the so-called prior's room lies over a vault in the western range.

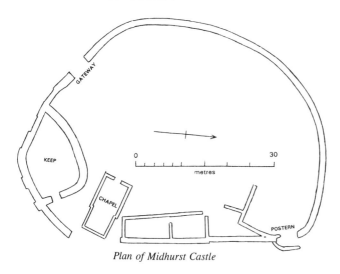

Plan of Midhurst Castle

MIDHURST   SU 889214   F

In 1913 the foundations of this castle were exposed by excavation, partly rebuilt, and left on show. A few moulded fragments then recovered suggested a mid 12th century date. Henry I granted Midhurst to Saveric Fitzcane and it was probably his son Geldwin who built a stone castle upon St Anne's hill. The dedication refers to an chapel, probably of 11th century date, standing on the east side of the site and having a nave and smaller chancel, both of them almost square. The 1.4m thick curtain wall enclosing an ovoid court 60m by 45m neither joins up with the chapel or runs beyond it. Perhaps a projection of some sort once closed the 10m wide gap. North of this was a range of buildings 18m long by 4.5m wide internally. Beyond are remains of other buildings and a projection probably containing a postern. South of the chapel was a keep of unusual form. A small and irregularly shaped court was created by a wall 1.5m thick curved round to cut off the SE end of the main court. The outer wall here has several broad buttresses of slight projection. West of the keep is a 4.6m wide gap representing the entrance, once narrower, presumably.

Midhurst Castle: View looking south towards the chapel

Midhurst Castle: The curtain wall

Saveric Fitzcane's son Frank took the surname de Bohun and this family held the manor until the 1490s. However they transferred to nearby Cowdray after the castle and another "messuage" (probably nearby Todham) were both dismantled by officers of the Earl of Arundel in 1311-15 whilst he had custody of the heir John Bohun, then a minor. When the earl was summoned to the King's Bench to account for this in 1316 the damage to the estate was said to be worth £1,000. The earl escaped punishment, claiming he was absent on military service in Scotland at the time.

Midhurst Castle: The walls of the keep

MILTON   TQ 530042

A natural ridge beside a now almost dry former loop of the Cuckmere River has been scarped into a low motte with a bailey to the north.

MOUNT CABURN   TQ 444089   F

The rampart of this large circular Iron Age hillfort high above Glynde was given a weak new palisade in the medieval period, perhaps to serve as a fortified village.

PERCHING   TQ 244116

In 1260, 1264, and 1268 Henry III issued licences for the manor house to be fortified, and another licence was granted to Sir Robert de Ardelme by Edward II in 1329. Traces of a moat lie 270m west of the Georgian farmhouse. The house passed in 1412 to Robert Poynings and then later went to Sir Anthony Browne.

PETWORTH   SU 977219

Henry de Percy, who erected much of the celebrated castle of Alnwick in Northumberland between 1309 and his death in 1315, obtained a licence from Edward II in 1309 to crenellate his manor house at Petworth. From the medieval period there now remain only a chapel of the 1260s, splendidly altered and refurnished in 1690-2, and the hall undercroft with a groin vault with thick octagonal piers. There must have been a moat and there may also have been a curtain wall and towers for Petworth is called a castle in Elizabeth I's reign. During that period extra apartments were added by Henry Percy, 8th Earl of Northumberland, who died in the Tower of London in 1585. Work continued under his son Henry, 9th Earl, who also languished for periods in the Tower of London, his brother Thomas being executed for his part in the Gunpowder Plot to kill James I in 1605. The 11th Earl died at Turin in 1670 and the Percy estates passed to an heiress who married Charles, 6th Duke of Somerset. In 1688 most of the medieval and Tudor work at Petworth was swept away for a huge new mansion on which work continued until 1696. There was some redecoration after a fire in 1714, a sculpture gallery was added at the north end c1780, outbuildings and stables were added at various periods during the 18th and 19th centuries, and the south front was remodelled to a design by Salvin in 1869-72.

The chapel at Petworth

The Roman walls of the outer ward at Pevensey

The inner ward at Pevensey

The east gate of the outer ward at Pevensey

PEVENSEY   TQ 645048   E

Pevensey was one of the forts of Saxon Shore built by the Romans probably in the early 4th century. The Pevensey fort may be the latest of the series and is more irregularly shaped, having a wall 3.6m thick and 7m high to the wall-walk surrounding a ten acre oval 280m long by 150m wide with a slight drop to what was originally the shoreline on the south. By the early 5th century the place was abandoned by the Romans. The Anglo-Saxon Chronicle records a massacre of Britons by the Saxons at Pevensey in 491 but excavations have found no evidence to corroborate this.

William I granted Pevensey to his half brother Robert de Mortain and the fort then became the outer bailey of a timber castle built within its SE corner. The Roman walls were then still fairly intact except on the south where they had been destroyed by subsidence. In 1088 Odo, Bishop of Bayeux held Pevensey against William II and the castle was only surrendered after the garrison ran out of provisions. After William, Count of Mortain joined Robert de Bellesme's rebellion against Henry I in 1101 Pevensey was forfeited and given by the king to Richard de Aquila. It was probably he who built the keep. Gilbert de Clare, Earl of Pembroke was besieged here by King Stephen in 1147 and again only famine caused the garrison to surrender. Stephen then gave Pevensey to his son Eustace.

The gatehouse of the inner ward at Pevensey

In 1154-5 Henry II obtained possession of the castle and returned it to Gilbert de Aquila. His namesake grandson sided with Louis of France against King John and Pevensey was forfeited but Henry III restored the castle to him. It was probably this Gilbert de Aquila who built the gatehouse in the 1220s. In the 1230s his heir sided with the French and Pevensey passed to Peter de Pivallis, then to the de Bohun Earl of Hereford, and then to Gilbert Marshall, Earl of Pembroke. In 1246 Henry III granted Pevensey to Peter of Savoy, Earl of Richmond and uncle of Queen Eleanor. He built the curtain wall and towers of the inner bailey before retiring to Savoy. By this time the outer bailey had probably been abandoned militarily following the collapse of a 50m section of the Roman wall on the north side. The removal of a chapel in the inner bailey to the outer bailey so that it would be more accessible for parishioners confirms this. In 1264 some of Henry III's forces fleeing from their defeat at Lewes took refuge in the castle. They were besieged by the younger Simon de Montfort but managed to hold out despite a length of wall being pulled down by the attackers.

After the conflicts of the 1260s Pevensey was held for a century by successive queen consorts and was often neglected, since they had many other residences. In 1306 it was reported that the constable had sold the wood of the dismantled timber bridge at the entrance and that a barn had collapsed and the wood had been used for fires. Subsequent reports note the collapse of the roof and floors of the north tower and the fall of the steps up to the keep entrance plus the dangerous state of its floors and roofs, while a section of the outer wall on the NE was ready to collapse in 1318. The castle was given by Edward III in 1372 to his son John of Gaunt, Duke of Lancaster but again was probably little used by him. In 1399 Lady Joan Pelham successfully defended the castle against Richard II after her husband Sir John had gone to join forces with John of Gaunt's son Duke Henry. After the latter became King Henry IV with the deposition of Richard II soon afterwards he showed his gratitude by granting Pevensey to Sir John Pelham. At Pevensey Sir John successively had custody of James I, King of Scotland, captured at sea by the English in 1406, and then Henry IV's widow Queen Joan, who was accused by her stepson Henry V of witchcraft. The roofs seem to have been maintained until the mid 15th century but the castle was then probably abandoned.

In 1573 the castle was noted as being too ruinous to be repaired but it seems to have been at least partly refortified in response to the threat of Armada in 1587. The gun platform in the middle of the south side of the outer ward probably dates from them. William III gave Pevensey to the Bentinck family but they sold the castle to the Earl of Wilmington. In 1782 it passed to the Duke of Devonshire. It was given to the Office of Works for preservation as a monument in 1925 but the war began before repairs and excavations were complete. In 1940 the castle was taken over by the army as an observation and command post, the towers being re-floored and roofed to accommodate troops, pillboxes for machine guns being erected on the keep and Roman bastions, and a blockhouse against tanks placed in the Roman west gate. The ruins are now in the custody of English Heritage.

Ariel view of Pevensey Castle

The west gate at Pevensey Castle

Although rather defaced on the inner side, the west, NW, east and NE portions of the Roman walls still stand almost complete. Originally they were flanked by fourteen bastions of which five remain at each of the west and east ends, plus traces of others at each end of the long collapsed south side. The bastions were solid below the wall-walk level but had thinly walled guard rooms at that level, one bastion on the NE still having remains of one of these. The long north and south sides required fewer bastions for adequate flanking. On the west two of the bastions are placed about 9m apart to protect a gateway. The passage itself was flanked by guard rooms, now destroyed, and was set within the line of the curtain. A postern with a dog-leg passage pierced the wall just west of the collapsed section on the north side. The fallen parts of this still remain with two pill boxes of 1940 hidden amongst them. On the east is another gateway in the form of a simple archway. This led to the harbour in Roman times. The bastions here are more widely spaced and one placed roughly where the medieval inner bailey wall adjoined has vanished along with the adjoining sections of wall. Traces of a section of late 11th century walling closing off a gap caused by collapse at the SW corner used to be visible, and the bastion north of the east gate has at the top herringbone masonry from a repair of that period.

Tower of the inner ward at Pevensey

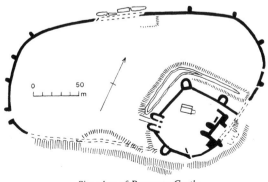

Site plan of Pevensey Castle

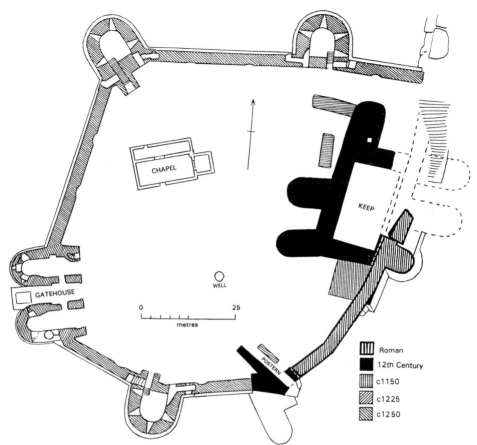

Plan of the inner ward of Pevensey Castle

The medieval castle measures about 80m across in each direction and has a water filled moat on the north and west. Apart from the section of Roman wall forming its east side, the earliest parts are the postern gate with a very long passage on the south side, the foundations of a chapel consisting of a nave, north aisle and square chancel in the middle of the bailey, plus the keep on the east side, all probably of c1105-25. The keep has a shape which is unique in Britain. Essentially an irregularly laid out rectangle of 24m by 17m over ashlar faced walls up to 3.3m, it had six apsidal shaped projections placed very irregularly. One was formed from a Roman bastion. The others were larger, being up to 6m wide with a projection of up to 9m. All were solid at the lowest level, where there were no lighting loops at all, but the projections probably contained chambers at the destroyed upper levels since one on the north contains a well shaft. The east side of the keep has collapsed and very little remains of two projections on this side. The block 10m by 8m added shortly afterwards against the south wall may have contained the principal private chambers on the upper levels. The entrance was always at the level of the hall on the second storey. Originally perhaps set between the western projections, in later times it was set at the NW corner, where later walls there helped carry an external stair up to it.

On the west side of the bailey is a gatehouse probably of the 1220s with a long passage flanked by U-shaped towers 8m wide. The causeway with a drawbridge pit immediately in front of the entrance is early 15th century. Not much of the southern tower stands above the level of the prison below passage level reached by a spiral stair on the south side. The northern tower has an oubliette or pit prison reached only by a trapdoor in the floor of a guardroom with three arrow loops. Two upper storeys were reached by a stair direct from the court at the NE corner. The curtain walls of the 1250s are 2.8m thick above a battered plinth and have several fireplaces which are all that remains of ranges of timber framed domestic buildings on all sides of the court. The wooden hall built in 1302 is thought to have been on the north side. At the NW corner and on the north and south sides are three D-shaped towers 11.2m wide above the plinths. The towers were all similar in arrangements. Each had a room reached directly from the court and having four arrow-loops towards the field and a latrine by the entrance. Below was a dark (and damp, being at moat level) basement reached from the court be a long straight flight of steps off which another passage led out to a postern. Above was an upper room with a fireplace reached only from the wall-walk, to which no original means of access now survives although recently a stairway has been provided to the NW tower upper level. The floors and roofs provided in 1940 still remain, although there is no glass in the windows. In the middle of the court is a well lined with masonry to a depth of 15m. Beside it is a pile of stone balls used by mangonels or trebuchets, relics of one of the sieges.

The inner gatehouse at Pevensey Castle

Motte at Pulborough

PULBOROUGH   TQ 037189   V

On an isolated hill commanding good views
0.5km west of Pulborough church is a tree-
covered motte rising 7m above a ditch with a
counterscarp bank. The very damaged NW side
of the motte faces towards a bailey platform
surrounded by a ditch.

RACKHAM   TQ 050125   V

Up on Rackham Hill beside the South Downs Way
is an enclosure built against an older dyke,
possibly part of the blockading arrangements
against Arundel in 1102.

RINGMER   TQ 449143

This is a damaged rectangular ringwork with a
rampart most prominent on the SW which faces
higher ground.

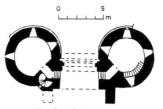

The Landgate at Rye

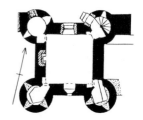

The Ypres Tower at Rye

RYE TQ 923203 O

The town of Rye occupies a natural defensive site, a sandstone plateau rising 15m above what was once a flourishing port. The History of the Dukes of Normandy mentions a castle here in 1216 but nothing remains of it. In 1249 Henry III ordered the Constable of the Cinque Ports, Peter of Savoy, to build a castle here as a defence against French raids. The small building standing on the south side of the town, now known as the Ypres Tower but originally called Baddings Tower, was the result. In the 1330s Edward III granted funds for the erection of stone walls around the town. Fragments of these survive on the north side and around the NW corner, together with one quite impressive gateway. Known as the Landgate it has an archway 4.2m wide with a portcullis groove and a pair of round flanking towers 6.4m in diameter over walls 1.4m thick. Only the bottom course remains of a machicolated parapet protecting the archway. The lowest rooms in the towers each have two loops towards the field and are reached from the gateway passage. One has a spiral staircase adjoining. A French raid in 1339 found the new defences inadequate, and in 1377 the town was again occupied by the French, the wooden houses being burnt and the inhabitants killed. Since the town hall was destroyed in this raid Baddings Tower was used by the Corporation for meetings and business until in 1430 it was sold off to John de Ypres, from whom the tower takes its present name.

The Landgate at Rye

The Ypres Tower at Rye

The Corporation of Rye rented the Ypres Tower for use as a prison from 1494 and in 1518 purchased it for £26. It remained in use as the town prison able to take 12 prisoners until downgraded to the status of a lock-up as a result of the 1865 Prison Act. It only ceased to be used for keeping prisoners when a new police station was erected in 1891. By then the lowest storey had become a mortuary, serving as such until 1959. From 1923 the tower was an ancient monument open to the public and from since the 1950s it has been a museum. It was re-roofed after suffering bomb damage in the 1940s. The tower has three storeys, the lowest being below the level of the ground to the north and having an inserted doorway on the west. Originally it was probably reached by a trapdoor. The tower is 7.5m square over walls 1.5m thick. Each corner has a round turret 3.8m in diameter, three of them containing small round rooms with narrow loops lower down and wider windows high up, whilst the NE turret contains a spiral stair linking the top two levels with the entrance at its foot.

The Ypres Tower at Rye

The interior of the Landgate at Rye

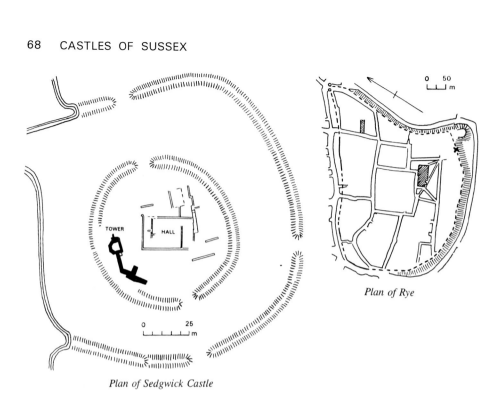

Plan of Rye

Plan of Sedgwick Castle

SEDGWICK   TQ 180270

The Sauvage family held Sedgwick from at least 1205 until 1249 when Robert Sedgwick, Sheriff of Sussex, transferred the manor to John Maunsell, Treasurer of York. In 1258 Henry III licensed John Maunsell to provide the house with ditches and crenellated walls of stone and lime. A second similar licence was issued in 1262 and from this period are assumed to date the ditch 9m wide surrounding a circular platform 50m across, on the west side of which are the much overgrown lower parts of two facets of a polygonal curtain wall 1.5m thick with a tower about 6m wide with a latrine on the south side and a polygonal west end. The ditch was probably dry since it lies at a higher level on the east than on the west. It is surrounded by an outer platform dropping down to a lake on the west and NW but having an outer ditch 9m wide on the other sides. On the east the land beyond this ditch is 9m higher than the level of the lake and the outer platform is itself 3m higher than the inner platform so the curtain would have needed to be quite lofty to adequately screen off this weak side. In 1263 the castle was held for the rebel barons by Peter de Montfort. The de Braose family obtained Sedgwick in an exchange of manors in the 1270s. After the last of this family died in 1395 the castle passed to Sir William Heron, and then to the Mowbrays. Excavations in 1923 found remains of considerable 15th century additions to a wide 11th century central hall block, probably timber framed. The Howard Dukes of Norfolk held Sedgwick from 1498 but rarely used it. From 1576 the castle was leased to Sir Thomas Fynes, and from 1602 it was leased to Sir John Caryll. In 1613 he dismantled the castle and used materials from it to build a new house to the east. In the early 19th century hundreds of cart loads of stone are said to have been taken from the castle ruins for the repair of local roads.

SELSEY   SZ 872957   V

The earthwork beside the church at Church Norton was thought to be an Elizabethan battery until excavation demonstrated it was part of a medieval ringwork.

VERDLEY   SU 903258

As a result of demolition for materials in 1880 hardly anything now remains of a rectangular building 20m long by 10m wide over walls 1.8m thick containing triangular-headed openings. The site lies at the foot of a slope and had a surrounding ditch. It is thought to have been a hunting seat of the de Bohuns.

UDIMORE   TQ 863180

The Norman church and adjoining buildings lie within two moated enclosures. In 1479 Edward IV granted a licence for crenellating a manor house here.

WALDRON   TQ 544192 and 560205

There is a circular moated platform in woodland west of Waldron church. A ditch remains of a possible motte 1.5km NE of the church.

WARNINGCAMP   TQ 030068

SW of Warningcamp crossroads are very slight traces of a platform with a bank on one side. It has given its name to the hamlet and is assumed to be one of Henry I's siege-works built to blockade Arundel Castle opposite in 1102.

The Pipewell Gate at Winchelsea

The Strand Gate at Winchelsea

WINCHELSEA   TQ 905175   V

In 1280 Edward I obtained the manor of Iham on the west side of the Rother with the purpose of founding a new town of Winchelsea. This was to replace the original settlement further east which, together with Rye, had become one of the Cinque Ports by 1191, but was devastated by storms, particularly in 1252, and by the conflicts between Henry III and his barons in the 1260s. The roughly triangular plateau was laid out with a regular grid of roads at the north end. Although the primary purpose of the new town was trade in Gascon wine it was given a ditch on the west, the only natural weak side, and three gateways. A castle was planned but never actually begun, probably because of the great expense of the king's castle building programme in North Wales. The town never developed as intended and although there are many medieval wine cellars remaining not much else medieval remains above ground apart from the three gates, the large but never finished church of St Thomas and the eastern part of the Franciscan friary church. The gates are quite modest, have little military character, and may be as late as 1415, when Henry V granted a licence for fortifying a smaller area than that originally laid out in 1283. The most impressive is the Strand Gate on the east, a rectangle of 6.4m by 4.4m over walls 0.8m thick with round turrets 2.8m in diameter at the corners. The passage was once covered by a rib-vault and was closed at each end by a portcullis. At ground level the corner turrets are solid except for a small round porter's lodge in the NE turret, but they all contained rooms at the upper level. The Pipewell Gate on the north is a rectangle of 7m by 6m with one upper room over a vaulted passage which was closed by two-leaved doors. The New Gate at the south end some way from the centre is an even more modest rectangular building with side-arches joining it to thin walls adjoining it at sharp angles. Little now remains of the upper room.

Plan of Pipewell Gate

Plan of Strand Gate

Plan of New Gate

New Gate at Winchelsea

Tower at Rymans, Apuldram

GLOSSARY OF TERMS

ASHLAR - Masonry of blocks with even faces and square edges. BAILEY - Defensible court enclosed by a wall or a palisade and ditch. BARBICAN - Defensible court, passage or porch in front of an entrance. BASTION - A projection rising no higher than the curtain wall. BRATTICE - A covered wooden gallery at the summit of a wall for defending its base. CORBEL - A projecting bracket to support other stonework or a timber beam. CURTAIN WALL - A high enclosing stone wall around a bailey. DEMI-BASTION - Bastion flanking just one side of the enceinte instead of two. EMBATTLED - Provided with a a parapet with indentations (crenellations). FOUR-CENTRED ARCH - An arch drawn with four compass points, two on each side. GUNPORT -an embrasure suitable for the discharge of heavy cannon. JAMB - A side of a doorway, window or other opening. KEEP - A citadel or ultimate strongpoint. The term is not medieval and such towers were then called donjons, from which word is derived the word dungeon meaning a prison. LIGHT - A compartment of a window. LOOP - A small opening to admit light or for the discharge of missiles. MACHICOLATION - A slot for dropping or firing missiles at assailants. MERLONS - The upstanding portions of a parapet. MOAT - A defensive ditch, water filled or dry. MOTTE - A steep sided flat-topped mound, partly or wholly man-made. OILLET - Small circular hole. PARAPET -A wall for protection at any sudden drop. PLINTH - The projecting base of a wall. It may be battered (sloped) or stepped. PORTCULLIS - A wooden gate made to rise and fall in vertical grooves, being hoisted by a windlass above. POSTERN - A back entrance or lesser gateway. RINGWORK - An embanked enclosure of more modest size than a bailey, generally of greater width but less elevated than a motte summit. SHELL KEEP - A small stone walled court built upon a motte or ringwork. SOLAR - A private living room for the lord and his family. TOWER HOUSE - Self contained defensible house with the main rooms stacked vertically. WALL-WALK - A walkway on top of a wall, always protected by a parapet. WARD - A stone walled defensive enclosure.

PUBLIC ACCESS TO THE SITES Codes used in the gazetteers.

E Buildings in the care of English Heritage. Fee payable at some sites.
F Sites to which there is free access at any time.
H Buildings currently used as hotels, restaurants, shops (free access to outside).
O Buildings opened to the public by private owners, local councils, National Trust.
V Buildings closely visible from public roads, paths, churchyards & open spaces.

FURTHER READING

The Buildings of Sussex, Ian Nairn & Nikolaus Pevsner, 1965
The Victoria County History of Sussex, several volumes, various dates.
A History of the King's Works, several volumes, 1963-70.
Norman Castles in Britain, Derek Renn, 1968
Castles in Sussex, John Guy, 1984
Pamphlet guides are available for Arundel, Bodiam, Bramber, Hastings, Lewes, Pevensey, and the Ypres Tower at Rye
Sussex Archeological Collections
See also periodicals such as Fortress, Medieval Archeology and Country Life.